COURAGEOUS LIFE AND LEGACY OF JELENA DOKIC

A Story of Triumph, Trauma, and Transformation

CALISTA MOON

All rights reserved. No part of this book may be reproduced, distributed, or transmitted in any form or by any means, including photocopying, recording, or other electronic or mechanical methods, without the prior written permission of the copyright owner except in the case of brief quotations embodied in critical reviews and certain other noncommercial uses permitted by copyright.

Copyright © 2024 by Calista Moon

Table of Contents

Chapter 1: Early Struggles and Rise in Tennis

Chapter 2: The Impact of Damir Dokic

Chapter 3: Enduring Abuse and Finding Resilience

Chapter 4: Breaking Free and Attempting a Comeback

Chapter 5: Legacy of Strength and Transformation

Conclusion

Chapter 1: Early Struggles and Rise in Tennis

Jelena Dokic was born in Osijek, Croatia, in 1983, during a time of deep-rooted political tensions in Eastern Europe. The Yugoslav Wars erupted when she was just a young child, creating a chaotic environment that her family would struggle to survive. The constant threat of violence and displacement deeply affected her family, driving them to search for a stable future away from their homeland. Her family eventually fled the war-torn region, leaving behind friends, memories, and their sense of home. This experience of displacement and uncertainty profoundly shaped Jelena's resilience and inner strength, qualities that would define her journey in tennis. Through these early adversities, she developed a mindset attuned to survival, which became an essential trait as she faced further personal battles both on and off the court.

A New Life in Australia

The Dokic family settled in Sydney, Australia, in the early 1990s, seeking refuge and a fresh start. For Jelena, Australia represented the hope of a stable life, but the challenges of immigration were significant. As a young girl adjusting to a new country, language, and culture, Jelena often felt isolated and alienated. Yet, she found comfort in the game of tennis, which became her outlet for expression and a tool for integration. This passion quickly developed into something more serious, as her talent on the court became apparent to both her family and tennis coaches. Her father, Damir, saw tennis as a potential pathway to success, and from a young age, Jelena dedicated herself fully to the sport. This drive was fueled by her determination to succeed in her new country and to bring her family pride and stability.

Rising Star in Junior Tennis

Jelena's extraordinary talent on the court was unmistakable. She started competing in junior tournaments, and it quickly became clear that she was a natural athlete. Her early matches showcased a strong and agile playing style, combined with a mental toughness uncommon for her age. By age 12, she was dominating local junior tournaments in Australia, catching the eye of prominent tennis coaches and scouts. Her skill set her apart from other young players, and she soon became recognized as a potential rising star in the Australian tennis community. She progressed through junior rankings, impressing with her powerful baseline play and an aggressive style that often overwhelmed her opponents. These early successes laid the foundation for what would soon be a meteoric rise in the world of professional tennis.

Defeating Martina Hingis at Wimbledon

At just 16 years old, Jelena made her senior Grand Slam debut at Wimbledon in 1999. The tournament was expected to be a learning experience, but she shocked the world by defeating the then-world No. 1, Martina Hingis, in straight sets. This victory against Hingis was one of the most significant upsets in Wimbledon history and instantly placed Jelena on the global tennis map. The match showcased her raw power, unwavering focus, and the tenacity she had developed over years of struggle. It was a defining moment, signaling her arrival in professional tennis and setting high expectations for her future. The win was not only a personal triumph but also a statement of her resilience—a young woman who had overcome war and displacement was now taking on and defeating the best in the world.

Damir Dokic's Influence

While Jelena's tennis career was rapidly ascending, her father's role in her life grew increasingly intense and controlling. Damir Dokic's belief in his daughter's talent was undeniable, but his methods were harsh and unyielding. He dictated nearly every aspect of her training, matches, and personal life, creating an environment of immense pressure. Damir's obsession with perfection meant Jelena rarely felt able to enjoy her achievements; each victory came with the expectation of more. His intense control and volatility began to cast a shadow over her accomplishments, making her early successes feel bittersweet. This complex relationship would not only affect her performance but also her personal development, planting the seeds for the struggles she would face later in her career.

After her breakthrough at Wimbledon, Jelena officially entered the world of professional tennis, joining the WTA tour and competing against seasoned players. She achieved several milestones, including reaching the semifinals at Wimbledon in 2000 and climbing to a career-high ranking of world No. 4 by 2002. Each achievement bolstered her reputation as a rising force in women's tennis, yet the challenges she faced off-court grew increasingly intense. Her father's influence, her internalized pressure to succeed, and the constant media scrutiny placed Jelena under immense strain. Despite these adversities, she continued to build her career with grit and determination, leaving a powerful mark in the tennis world. Her early years in the sport, filled with both triumph and tribulation, set the stage for her enduring legacy as a player who defied the odds.

Chapter 2: The Impact of Damir Dokic

The relationship between Jelena Dokic and her father, Damir Dokic, is one of the most complex and challenging aspects of her journey in professional tennis. Damir's intense, often volatile influence over Jelena's career affected nearly every aspect of her personal and professional life, casting a long shadow over her success. While he played an instrumental role in shaping her as an athlete, his controlling and frequently abusive behavior became a major source of trauma for Jelena, both during her career and well into her adult life.

Early Role in Jelena's Tennis Development

Damir saw Jelena's potential in tennis at an early age and dedicated himself to developing her as a player, pushing her to train intensely from the time they moved to Australia. He saw tennis as a way to achieve financial stability and social standing, as well as a path out of the difficulties their family had faced in the aftermath of the Yugoslav Wars. His relentless drive for Jelena to succeed became all-consuming, shaping her childhood and adolescence around the demands of the sport. While many athletes benefit from strong parental support, Damir's approach was harsh and unwavering, focused solely on victory and not on Jelena's personal well-being or happiness.

Under Damir's guidance, Jelena quickly rose through the junior ranks and caught the attention of the tennis world. His methods, however, were often extreme, and his demanding nature meant that Jelena had little freedom to enjoy her achievements or experience life outside of her career. Her father's high expectations created an environment where even her most impressive successes were rarely celebrated but viewed as mere stepping stones to further accomplishments. Damir's influence kept Jelena under intense scrutiny, laying a foundation for the internal pressure and stress that would haunt her in the years to come.

The Downward Spiral of Control and Abuse

As Jelena's career advanced, Damir's methods became increasingly harsh and invasive. His role in her life shifted from that of a supportive parent to a figure of intense control, dictating every aspect of her personal and professional choices. Damir became infamous for his outbursts and erratic behavior at tournaments, which attracted significant media attention and, at times, even led to his ejection from events. His reputation as a difficult figure in the tennis world began to precede him, overshadowing Jelena's accomplishments on the court. She often had to contend with the added challenge of being associated with her father's controversies, which distracted from her achievements and put her under additional stress.

Jelena has openly described the abuse she endured under her father's influence, revealing that his controlling behavior was not just limited to her tennis career but extended into all areas of her life. This abusive dynamic created a traumatic environment that left her feeling trapped and helpless. The emotional toll on Jelena was severe, impacting her self-esteem, mental health, and, ultimately, her performance. While she continued to rise in the tennis ranks, the personal cost of her success was profound.

Breaking Free and Reclaiming Her Independence

In 2002, Jelena made the difficult decision to separate herself from her father's influence, a decision that marked a turning point in her life and career. The choice was fraught with challenges, as her father's presence had been a constant since the beginning of her tennis journey. She had to confront the psychological impact of years of abuse and the fear that she might lose her career without his support. However, breaking free from her father allowed Jelena to start building her identity outside of his control, giving her a chance to experience a sense of agency for the first time in years. This period of independence was a critical step toward healing, though the scars of her father's control would remain with her.

The Long-Term Effects on Jelena's Career and Personal Life

The impact of Damir's control left a lasting mark on Jelena's career and personal life. The years of constant stress, fear, and self-doubt had taken their toll, and she struggled to regain her confidence and stability. Damir's abusive behavior had not only affected her emotional health but also eroded her love for the sport. Despite her tremendous talent and early success, Jelena's career trajectory was deeply affected by the trauma she endured. Even after separating from her father, she faced an uphill battle in finding consistent success on the tour, as the psychological wounds hindered her ability to perform at her best.

Bringing Awareness to Abuse in Sports

In the years following her retirement, Jelena has become an outspoken advocate for awareness of abuse within the sports world. Her memoir reveals the depth of her father's influence and the impact of his behavior, shedding light on the darker side of parental involvement in competitive sports. Her story has resonated with many who have experienced similar struggles, sparking conversations about the need for safeguards and support systems for young athletes. Through her advocacy, Jelena has transformed her personal pain into a powerful message, helping others understand the importance of creating a nurturing environment in sports.

Legacy and Moving Forward

While Jelena's relationship with her father cast a long shadow over her career, her courage in confronting and sharing her story has given her a new sense of purpose. By reclaiming her narrative, she has redefined her legacy, highlighting her resilience and determination. Her journey stands as both a cautionary tale and a testament to the human spirit's capacity for healing. Despite the profound challenges imposed by her father, Jelena's impact on tennis and her advocacy against abuse serve as an enduring reminder of her strength, making her journey one of both triumph and transformation.

Chapter 3: Enduring Abuse and Finding Resilience

Jelena Dokic's story is one of resilience in the face of unimaginable hardship. From her early years in tennis, she was forced to endure a level of abuse that went far beyond the pressures typically associated with competitive sports. The emotional and physical toll of her father's abuse was profound, impacting her both on and off the court. Yet, through sheer willpower and determination, she continued to push forward, maintaining a level of strength that allowed her to rise through the tennis ranks and achieve significant success. This journey, marked by endurance and inner resilience, is a testament to Jelena's strength and serves as a powerful example of overcoming adversity.

The abuse Jelena endured at the hands of her father, Damir Dokic, was both physical and psychological. Damir's control over her was relentless, shaping every aspect of her life with an oppressive intensity. He monitored her diet, training regimen, social life, and even her thoughts. His unpredictable and often violent outbursts created an environment of fear and anxiety. Jelena has recounted how her father's anger would erupt in both verbal and physical abuse, leaving her constantly on edge. This toxic dynamic extended beyond their home, affecting her experiences on the tennis court as well. Damir's high expectations meant that even when Jelena performed well, it was never good enough; each win was met with new demands, and each loss with harsh punishment.

For a young athlete, this level of pressure and fear was overwhelming. The normal stresses of competing on an international level were compounded by her father's abusive behavior, making each match feel like a matter of survival rather than a career milestone. Jelena felt trapped in a cycle of trying to meet her father's demands and fearing his reaction if she failed. This pattern of abuse, compounded over years, took a profound toll on her mental and physical well-being, often leaving her feeling isolated and hopeless.

Mental and Physical Toll of the Abuse

Enduring such sustained abuse took a severe toll on Jelena's mental health. She often felt like she had no escape from her father's control, and the constant pressure to succeed at all costs created feelings of anxiety, depression, and self-doubt. She began to internalize her father's criticisms, questioning her worth and capabilities. In her memoir, she describes how this abuse stripped away her confidence and left her feeling emotionally numb. The psychological trauma affected her ability to enjoy her success, as victories felt hollow under her father's oppressive influence.

The physical abuse also had a direct impact on her tennis career. Damir's intense training methods and demands often led Jelena to push her body beyond its limits, resulting in injuries that affected her performance. Furthermore, the physical abuse she experienced at home drained her energy and left her physically weakened, making it difficult to compete at her best. Despite these challenges, Jelena persevered, often relying on her love for tennis to sustain her through the darkest moments.

Finding Resilience Amidst Trauma

Jelena's resilience in the face of this trauma is a testament to her incredible inner strength. Despite the physical and emotional toll of her father's abuse, she continued to train and compete at an elite level. For Jelena, tennis was not just a career but also an escape—a way to channel her pain and assert her own identity in a life dominated by her father's control. The court became a place where she could express herself and briefly distance herself from the abuse she faced at home. This resilience allowed her to maintain a high standard of performance, even when everything else in her life felt uncertain.

Jelena's determination to persevere also extended to her efforts to seek support, though these were often met with obstacles. She tried reaching out to others in her life for help, but the taboo nature of familial abuse in sports often left her feeling unheard. The shame and stigma associated with admitting her father's abusive behavior made it difficult to find allies who could help her navigate her situation. Nevertheless, she continued to push forward, driven by a desire to succeed despite the odds stacked against her.

Breaking Free and Rebuilding

Over time, Jelena began to recognize that escaping her father's influence was the only way to regain control of her life.

Her decision to distance herself from Damir marked a critical step toward healing, though it was a journey fraught with difficulty. Breaking free from his control required confronting years of emotional trauma and finding ways to rebuild her confidence. This period of self-recovery allowed her to start redefining her identity outside of her father's control, giving her a newfound sense of independence.

Using Her Story as a Beacon of Hope

In recent years, Jelena has used her platform to speak out about her experiences, hoping to inspire others who might be facing similar situations. By sharing her story, she has helped bring awareness to the issue of abuse in sports, encouraging young athletes to seek help and reminding them that they are not alone. Her resilience in the face of prolonged abuse, and her willingness to share her journey, have become a source of inspiration for many, showcasing the power of resilience in overcoming adversity.

Chapter 4: Breaking Free and Attempting a Comeback

The decision to separate from her father marked a monumental turning point in Jelena Dokic's life and career. After enduring years of intense control and abuse, Jelena finally took the step to break free from Damir Dokic's influence, a decision that required immense courage and self-determination. This period was not only about gaining independence but also about reclaiming her life, her identity, and her love for tennis. For Jelena, this meant attempting a return to the professional tennis circuit, a daunting task given the emotional and physical toll her years of trauma had taken on her. Yet, despite the challenges, her journey to rebuild her career remains a powerful story of resilience and self-discovery.

Gaining Independence and Reclaiming Identity

Breaking free from her father's influence was a gradual process, fraught with emotional turmoil. Having been under Damir's control since she was a young teenager, Jelena's sense of identity was deeply entangled with his expectations and demands. Gaining independence meant redefining herself, not as her father's protege or a tennis prodigy forced to perform, but as an individual with her own aspirations and desires. In this process, Jelena had to confront the trauma she had endured, acknowledging the pain and allowing herself to heal.

Independence also meant handling the responsibilities that her father had previously controlled, from managing her training and finances to making her own career decisions. This newfound freedom was both exhilarating and overwhelming. Without her father's overbearing presence, Jelena experienced a mix of relief and uncertainty; she was finally free but also faced with the unknown. This transition period allowed her to reclaim her autonomy, finding joy in small moments and rediscovering her own motivations.

The Challenges of a Tennis Comeback

Returning to competitive tennis was not a straightforward path for Jelena. Having been absent from the circuit due to injury and her strained relationship with her father, Jelena faced a significant gap in her training and match readiness. Rejoining the professional ranks after such an extended hiatus required rigorous physical preparation, and Jelena had to push her body to recover the strength and agility necessary for elite competition. Furthermore, the injuries she had sustained from years of overtraining and mistreatment took a toll on her body, requiring her to take a cautious approach to training.

In addition to the physical demands, the mental strain of reentering such a high-pressure environment was substantial. Returning to a career so closely associated with her father's abuse meant that Jelena had to confront memories of trauma every time she stepped onto the court. Tennis was her passion, but it was also a painful reminder of the years she had spent under her father's oppressive control. Despite these challenges, Jelena was determined to prove to herself that she could play on her own terms. She began to focus on her personal goals, aiming to find fulfillment beyond just winning matches.

Emotional Hurdles and Finding Support

One of the most significant hurdles Jelena faced in her comeback was the need for emotional support. Rebuilding her career meant navigating an industry that had been complicit in ignoring the abuse she endured. She faced criticism from those who questioned her ability to perform after such a long break, while others still associated her with her father's volatile reputation. Seeking support, Jelena turned to friends, family members, and mentors who encouraged her to focus on her healing journey. These individuals provided a sense of stability that Jelena had not experienced before, allowing her to gain confidence and assurance that she was not alone.

Her comeback attempt also involved public scrutiny, with media attention often fixating on her past rather than her efforts to rebuild. Jelena had to learn to manage this attention, channeling her energy into her training and focusing on her well-being. Slowly, she began to establish boundaries, balancing her desire to share her story with the need to protect her mental health.

Competing on Her Own Terms

One of the most significant aspects of Jelena's comeback was the freedom to compete on her own terms. Without the constant pressure and interference of her father, she found herself able to focus on the enjoyment of the game rather than the relentless pursuit of victory. This shift in perspective allowed her to appreciate her achievements and setbacks, understanding that her worth was not tied solely to her performance on the court. For Jelena, competing was now about personal growth and the fulfillment of achieving goals she had set for herself, not her father's ambitions.

Though her comeback journey was challenging and did not lead to the same level of professional success she had achieved in her early years, Jelena's resilience became her legacy. Her story resonates with those who have faced adversity, showcasing the power of self-belief and the courage to rebuild after experiencing trauma. By breaking free from her father's influence, Jelena reclaimed her life, her voice, and her sense of purpose.

Her comeback, while marked by struggles, stands as a powerful symbol of hope and empowerment, inspiring others to pursue their passions on their own terms. Today, Jelena's legacy is not just as a tennis player, but as a survivor and an advocate for resilience, underscoring the importance of mental well-being, independence, and personal freedom.

Chapter 5 Legacy of Strength and Transformation

Jelena Dokic's legacy extends far beyond her achievements on the tennis court, resonating deeply as a story of strength and transformation. Emerging from a turbulent past marked by intense personal challenges, she has become a powerful symbol of resilience, inspiring countless survivors of abuse and adversity. Jelena's story illustrates not only her strength but also her commitment to transforming her pain into purpose, using her experiences to advocate for change in the often high-pressure world of sports.

As a former tennis prodigy, Jelena's early promise was overshadowed by a complex relationship with her father and coach, Damir Dokic. Breaking free from his control was a monumental step toward reclaiming her identity and sense of self-worth, an act that required immense bravery. Her journey has illuminated issues around mental health, athlete abuse, and the critical need for a supportive environment in sports. Jelena's openness about her struggles has brought attention to these issues, fostering a wider dialogue about the importance of athlete well-being.

Today, Jelena's impact continues as she works to support young athletes, helping to create a sports culture where mental health and personal dignity are prioritized. Her story serves as a beacon for those facing similar struggles, offering hope and encouragement. By sharing her journey of transformation, Jelena has left a lasting legacy that champions empathy, resilience, and the pursuit of positive change, both on and off the court.

Conclusion

Jelena Dokic's journey is a profound testament to resilience, determination, and the power of reclaiming one's life. From her rise as a young tennis prodigy to enduring years of abuse and control, she faced challenges that tested her spirit at every turn. Her career, marked by both exceptional victories and crushing obstacles, reflects not only her prowess on the court but her strength off it. Breaking free from her father's oppressive grip was a pivotal moment that allowed Jelena to pursue a life of her own choosing, though it came with its own battles of rebuilding and self-discovery.

Her courage in publicly sharing her story has made her an influential advocate for change, bringing attention to the often-hidden realities of abuse in sports and beyond. By doing so, she has empowered countless others to seek help, find their voice, and push for a culture that prioritizes the welfare of athletes.

Today, Jelena's legacy transcends her tennis accomplishments. It lies in her transformation from a victim of circumstance to a beacon of hope and resilience. She has become a symbol of strength, illustrating that one's past does not have to define their future. Through her advocacy and personal story, Jelena Dokic continues to inspire and foster positive change in sports and society at large, leaving an enduring impact that goes far beyond the tennis court. Her journey is a reminder that, with courage and determination, overcoming even the darkest moments is possible.

Printed in Great Britain
by Amazon

58371995R00030